FAITH

Poems and illustrations

by

Pauline Kirk

The Parish Church of St. Edward the Confessor,
Dringhouses, York

Published by the Parish Church of St. Edward the Confessor,
Dringhouses, York

Typeset by Pauline Kirk
Printed by Quacks, York

Copyright © Pauline Kirk 2006

ISBN: 0-9533851-1-6
        978-0-9533851-1-9

Some of these poems first appeared in the following journals and anthologies: *A Taste of the Pennine Poets, Aireings, Breaking Bread, Expressions of Faith, Gabriel, Loose Change, Mobius Poetry* (USA), *NASA* (USA), *New Hope International, New Hope International Pickings* (www.nhi.clara.net/pick.56.htm), *Pennine Platform, Pennine Poets Anthology 1966-86, Pennine Twenty Five, Pilgrimages, Poetry in the Parks, Poetry Opens Everyone's Minds and Senses, Poetry Monash* (Australia), *Q* (USA), *Reflections of War, Second Light Newsletter, Telling Tales, The Church News, The Poetry Church, The Third Half, The Poetry Church Collection Summer 2004, The World at our Feet, Twenty Lines, Ultra Koncise* (USA), *Webbed Skylights of Tall Oaks, Radio Leeds.*
Illustrations – front cover: Darby and Joan Party, Mumford, Kidderminster; back cover: Pauline Kirk by Peter Kirk; page 5: "USA Friend", courtesy of the Hill family, Birmingham. All other photographs are by Pauline Kirk.

CONTENTS

	Page
Advent	15
Benediction (for a wedding)	34
Brief Magic	26
Christmas Irreverents	16
Colosseum	14
Crocuses	26
Driftwood	8
Faith Tea	35
Feather	32
For Christina Rossetti	19
Hannah Noah Speaks	6
Hymn – God Gives…	32
Japanese Garden	21
Meditation	11
Mijas	30
Nativity Play	20
Outbreak of War	22
Pet Blessing	28
Photographs on a Pub Wall	5
Plague Village	12
Railway Line: Disused	4
Reflections	29
Refugees	24
San Vitale	9
Squirrel	8
War Cemetery	25
Yorkshire Nativity	17
Other Publications by the Author	36

Railway Line : Disused

When the archeologists come
to poke among our entrails,
what theory will they offer,
finding these rusted rails?

Already birch and elderberry grow.
Thistles from a nearby field
creep along the platform.
The gravel begins to yield.

No pride of steam roars along
this pointless track gasping fire.
Sleepers and ballast disappear,
Autumn lights a funeral pyre.

And will our motorways
one day bloom so, roots
forcing through concrete,
service stations sprouting shoots?

As the experts scrape a fly-over
what myth will they offer then?
Will they think our rails and roads
sacred lines drawn for Heaven

or theorise on ritual sacrifice?
They will need some explanation
for a race who conquered space and speed
but forgot the power of thistle seed.

Photographs on a pub wall

Eyes framed in gilded wood
criticise my evening drink.
A woman in hunting gear poses;
carters smoke reflective pipes.
Centre space on the far wall
(above the imitation fireplace)
a couple prepares to picnic,
bottle of wine and glasses
propped on a rickety stool.
Who were you all?

What lives, dreams,
lay behind each image,
caught for posterity
and to decorate a noisy pub?
No one answers my question
though a parade of beauty queens
stares back, unexplained.
Lord, let me not end so,
my life sold on a market stall -
pub decor to another age.

Hannah Noah speaks

Last year he swore the sun would tumble
and burn us all, then he dreamt the waves stopped
and fish froze solid. This spring, his fear was
a Great Flood. "The world will drown,"
he predicted, "every living thing."
I called him a fool and went to feed the goats.

Then I found him lugging trees down the cattle byre.
His eyes were hollows filled with light.
"I'm mekking a boat," he snarled -
the prow stretched right down our barn.
Nor could he rest until our sons had joined him.
Their hammers hurt my brain -
and the cows bellowing, wanting milking,
with only me aware.

I killed the goats on my own too, my hair
gobbed with blood. We must take one pair of all
our stock he said. The rest must be salted down.
So I hacked and chopped and boiled
and could not stop shivering.

The neighbours laughed as we passed,
until a plug fell out the clouds.
In an hour the drains were fountains.
By nightfall, water was crumbling our walls.
The lights died, but I could hear the terror next door
and how they scrambled for chairs and mats
anything that would float.

Noah was aflame then, shouting and praying
– useless. I had to grab the children and fill the water jars
and stack the food, and stop Shem's wife from screaming.
We forced a hundred hands away when we launched,
slithering down our lawn ...

My sister's face will always float before me.

Two weeks ago the rains stopped. Now
the great lake recedes. We creep between stumps of walls,
through mud and carcasses. Soon we must hit ground
and scramble to begin anew. It is easier to drift
with an acceptable routine. The silence hurts though;
a few bleatings, a cough or two, the creak of canvass …
little else. Even Noah has stopped asking, "Why us?"
just sits against the hay, watching the rainbow.

Perhaps others live beyond the rim of sky,
but though we watch hour upon hour,
no vessel passes us, on this vast, filthy sea.

Driftwood

How does so slight a shard
mellow to such beauty? -
lined with blue bands of horizon,
seascapes of grey, roofs of thin cloud.

Staring at this fragment of deck
I see seasons pressed like sand
layer upon layer. Those faint dots,
how they shape-shift too -

one moment, pockmarks
on the face of Time, another,
just an insect boring its meal.
The wood is silk-soft, smoothed

by an ocean's rolling. Yet,
like the art it unwittingly becomes,
this once bore men and women
above pitiless depths. When?

Ten, fifty years past, a thousand even.
And before that, the tree, and beyond then
the acorn .... The swing of the waves
cradles me towards Infinity.

Squirrel

Frozen by fear and car headlights,
You come to depend upon me,
Interfere with my plans. You have rights:
I cannot callously drive over you.
I must move you, it seems, bodily.
Half-vexed, half-amused, I leave my car,
Though the lane is lonely
And time pressing.

Your heart beats under my hand:
Your warmth surprises, reminds me
Of kittens and piglets and days on the land.
Apologising, I place you on a wall.
Suddenly, you find life. Your back arches,
Then you vanish into dusk.
For a moment, my city self pauses,
Envying the wild. All that evening,
Your heart beats on, under my hand.

San Vitale

This church is not in the guide book.
According to authority, there is nothing of worth
on Via Nazionale. Traffic thunders past our hotel,
fumes stain offices and clothing shops.
Yet each day we have passed these steps,
and been tempted downwards.

With only two hours left, we succumb,
and find a Roman basilica, sanctified.
San Vitale in Roma, last repaired
five or six centuries ago, and needing
urgent refurbishment, greets us.
The heavy door shuts out sun and traffic.

We enter a cool sanctuary,
scented and soft as an old woman's cheek.
Light settles on gold; a priest's voice flickers.
We are interlopers, northern Protestants
stumbling into early morning mass.
Silently we retreat, and close the door.

"I'll be back," I promise no one in particular.
Spanish steps, Colosseum, Vatican,
none have caught my love as quickly
as this unassuming basilica.
Six hours later, we are a thousand years away,
landing on grey tarmac, on an greyer afternoon.

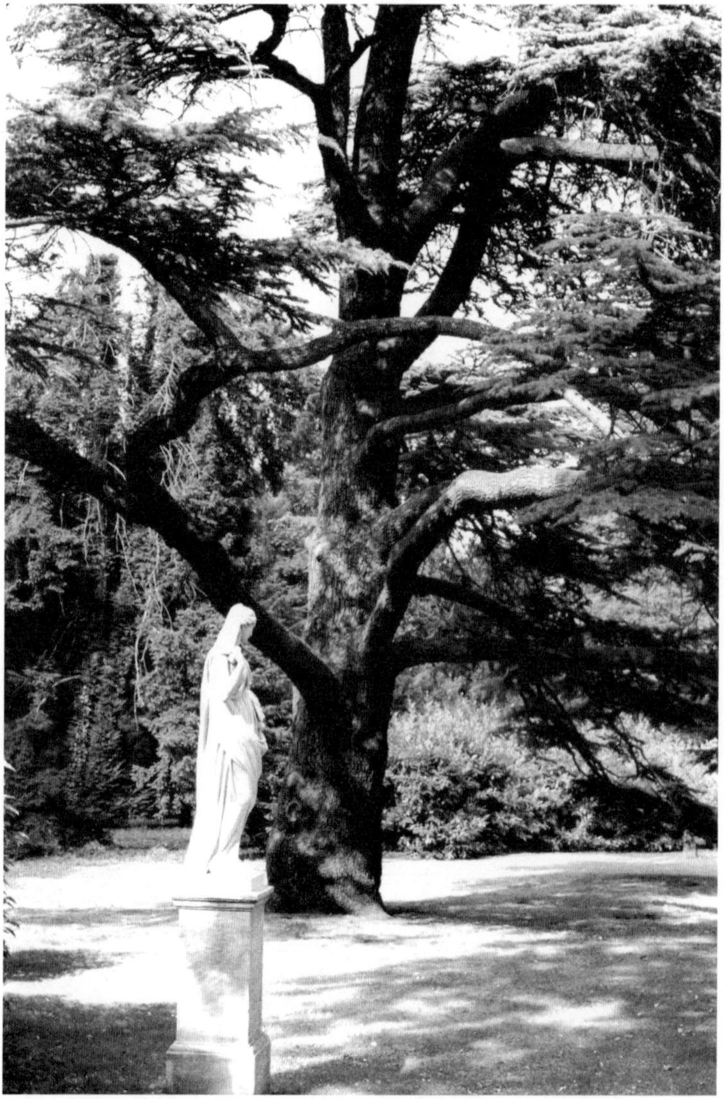

Meditation

Last night, while darning yet another sock,
I jerked the needle, and stabbed my female calm,
Till thoughts seeped through, from out of stock.
Unbidden, a chapel memory invited contrast,
Surprisingly religious. A nail would make
A bigger hole than that, I thought
If hammered through flesh,
Till bone and blood are past.
Ah, to submit to that, forgiving still
Why, the man must have been insane,
A deluded fool, his brain desert-ill.
No sensible fellow lets his flesh be torn.

The trouble is, others have chosen
Death as pointless, in lengthy pain.
Socrates drank his hemlock,
Joking as he sipped, and unyielding Joan
Sang on her funeral fire.
Were all mad, or all, including Christ,
Right? An odd thought.
Why should a god so aspire
To die by the evil of those he made?
Me? I'd have howled blue murder, tried
At least to make the odds more even,
For he too in the end cried.

Still, I am not Christ – thank Heaven.

Plague Village

Our schools study this place, write projects, or come on coaches
To view its church, the narrow streets, its stocks;
All Summer the cars arrive bringing after-dinner trippers;
They read the plaque and sigh before seeking antiques;
Eyam, plague village.

This Sunday a woman sits reading in a garden of roses
While passing crowds lean across her wall to seek the sign:
'Plague Cottages'. There – behind her – in those mellow houses
Deathly roses once bloomed, ring-a-ringing dying cheeks.
"George Viccars: September 7th. 1665."

Visitors gather round Mompesson's church,
Admire the ancient cross and loiter through the porch,
See his chair, and pause, gathering before an illumined page.
Sydall ... and Derby ... Hancock – Dear God, so many names ....
Eyam, plague village.

We leave for fresher air and stand amongst the flowers.
The trippers seek their coaches, beginning to chatter like sparrows,
Pleased with gifts and cards, pockets full of posies;
But we, being independent, stroll on past stone and roses,
Through a honied afternoon.

As directed, we raise a cover to observe a bull baiting ring,
Then, having eaten too much at lunch,
Decide on a green climbing path, through purple dead nettle
And wild white parsley, towards Mompesson's well, high above
Eyam, plague village.

An arrow directs us to a stone capped stream, where once goods
And food were left to aid a self-besieged community.
Afterwards I return alone, though with others, through woods
Those few survivors must have trudged.
Dear God, so many names ....

Would I have stayed? George the tailor thought he had a bargain
No doubt, but bought dear at any price, plague cash on delivery.
And those other folk who lived where the old lady reads, they shared
Like good neighbours and died, without choice, here in
Eyam, plague village.

But what of those men of God, William and Thomas? How did they
Persuade to a heroic death folk more used to cheating at cards
Or drinking porter? The waiting must have been worst, examining
Under arms, watching for graves appearing among the neighbour's hay
(Seven in Riley's field.)

Would I have stayed? Could I have stayed,
For the good of others waiting my own death here?
The merest cold, a scent of grass would have sent fear
Sneezing through my brain. Or would I, like the squire, have fled from
Eyam, plague village?

For me the word courage is defined in this narrow place,
In Mompesson and Stanley, in the story of Mistress Hancock
And her seven graves, and in you too gentle Emmott,
With your secret sweetheart and fresh country face.
How could you love

And not flee when Rowland called you to safety,
Across the rocks at Cucklett Delf? There would be no joy
To keep you that Christmas, no carols with the church shut,
No wreathes except on graves, and no one daring to kiss ...
Eyam, plague village.

Of three hundred and fifty villagers, two hundred and fifty nine ...
My modern mind will not focus, seeks comfort amongst the tourists
Until, seeing a plaque not noticed before, I cross to read the dead.
Bagshaw House: six here, and the last one Emmott Sydall.

Suddenly
I am crying, standing in a busy street.

Colosseum

We run for our lives between cars.
No one so much as swerves.
Owning so much time around
and beneath leaves too little for now.
Shaken, we stand in wonder,
beside a Colosseum, taller, wider
bolder than we imagined.
Seventy thousand people
could cheer while gladiators died,
then flow away, within ten minutes.
The tiers remain, but the marble seating
is gone, stolen to decorate palaces,
or simply to fill a hole.

A bronze cross recalls the martyrs,
condemned 'ad bestias',
death by entertainment.
Our guidebook disputes the number,
a mere three hundred perhaps,
but each death a terror of waiting
and a roaring crowd. Nero may even
have ordered Rome burnt
I read aloud, to build his Golden House
on land the flames had cleared –
and then blamed the Christians.
Every Fascist needs their fall-guy race.

My throat tightens.
In silence, we separate,
walking round the great circle
trying to gain some sense of scale.
Through the viewfinder,
my photograph of you waving
shows no more than a distant speck.

Advent

"Si-ii- lent Ni-ght"–
A thin wail of carol rises
from her daily stage, the doorway
where she performs, and earns a pound or so
in pennies. Behind her, the Minster broods,

golden for a season. Before her,
a fairyland flickers blue and silver
down Petergate, tinges her face as she plays,
more practised at 'Frere Jacques' than holiness.
Shoppers pass like frantic mice, too stressed

to notice her, or the sly mist that slinks
down lanes, round refuse bins, near mews
where a tired executive closes curtains
and hopes for a drunk free night.
Fingers almost too stiff to play

she repeats her faltering plea.
And still the feet rush past,
urgent to reach shops before they shut,
while from the market
a bootleg tape answers with 'Jingle Bells'.

Christmas Irreverents

I

Christmas is acoming
The streets are being lit.
Please put a twenty
In the Ad man's hat.
If you haven't got a twenty,
A Euro note will do,
If you haven't got a Euro
Then poor old you.

II

The first Nowell the radio blared
Was to certain poor housewives in shops as they fought;
In shops where they fought buying at eight
On a cold winter's night that was so late.
Nowell, nowell, nowell, nowell …
The tannoi drowns out "Isra –el".

III

While shop girls wrapped their socks in bags
All standing chewing gum,
A certain hardy Yorkshire lass
Came present-hunting glum.

"Push not!" said she, for mighty Joan
Had seized the camiknickers.
"I'm hevving the bloomin' lot
For Sharon and her nippers!"

IV

See amid the plastic snow –
Bought for you on tick you know.
See the game boy set appear
Promised since last New Year.
Hail thou long awaited morn!
Hail the parents' sleepy dawn.
Sing along with Wayne's modem.
Happy days on line for him.

Yorkshire Nativity

What strange scene is this?
Horses watch, sheep wait.
A man plods a narrow lane,
leading a donkey.
His tired wife rides.

This is Nativity,
Yorkshire style.
Cold stiffens hands,
snow and darkness settle.
There are no angels

just a shepherd or two,
well wrapped.
One has a mobile 'phone.
But the ambulance he calls
sticks wheel-deep,

so their shelter must be
a cattle-shed, their light
a frost-circled moon.
By morning, Mary
cradles a son.

Geese and shepherds
sing alleluia.

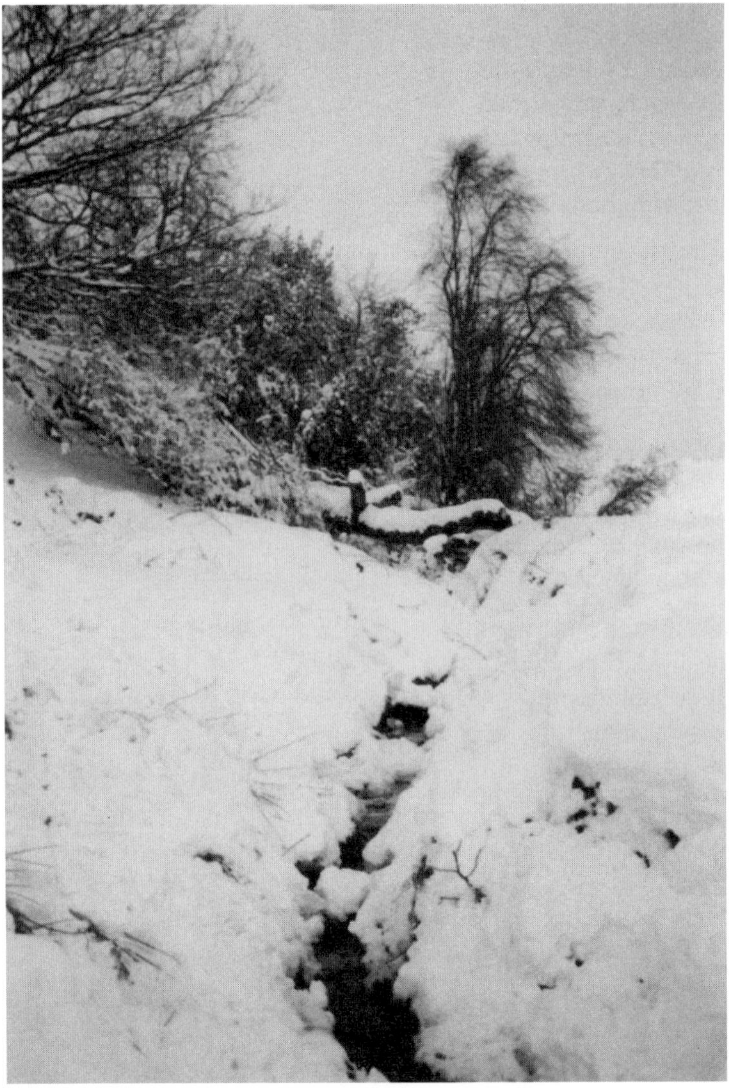

For Christina Rossetti *

We have no snow upon snow this year,
Just wind and rain and a blackened river.
In your day Midwinter was bleaker,
Before power stations and cars.
Yet your childhood sounds warmer than ours.
A gaiety of visiting émigrés heated your parlour;
You talked poetry with Grandfather Polidori,
Lent your face to brother Dante's art. No wonder
Your head hummed with singing birds and sprites.

I would not change with you, even so.
Only men could gain brotherhood of arts then,
However Pre-Raphaelite.
You were taught to come second, posed as virgin
Until you could play no other part.
Faith knitted you a thin comforter and you did your duty,
Cared for mother and aunts, hid your body in bombazine.
By the time cancer beat you, you must have wondered
If life was worth your song.

A hundred years on, two galleries are full of you.
Your features cover their walls.
As I walk into a London Winter, my mind
Sings your rhythms, your carols lift my soul.
Despite our differering times, we share so much:
A woman's conscience, mother, aunts...
Too little time for creation.
Suddenly, in my head, I am writing again.
After eight months' silence words bang at my brain.

Watching Christmas lights plait along the river,
I thank you, Christina, woman to woman.
Your bleak Midwinter has thawed my own.

* Writer of 'In the Bleak Midwinter' and other hymns

Nativity Play

First come the angels, trailing clouds of bathroom net
and glory, tinsel bright under a cooking foil star.
Hitching white night-dresses above small white feet
they climb an unsteady heaven, and wave, towards earthly mothers.

Next comes Mary, immaculate in borrowed curtains,
while behind a piano a shuffling choir sings lul-ley
and Joseph forgets his lines. A doll is born,
explaining in two seconds a two thousand year mystery;

we smile, until nervous shepherds bring lambs
to give on cue, and we manage a carol or two,
four wheeler Christians singing an annual apology.
Then from classroom palaces, kings appear.

They offer tea caddies and myrrh in a biscuit tin
but my thoughts have left them, travelling private deserts
to sit in a hospital ward, beside a dignified, dying man.
Returning, I find a troop of grenadiers in crepe paper,

each tapping my grief on a sweet nostalgic drum.
"Tar-rump-pap-pum-pum" they play, "What shall I give him?
Ta-rump-pap-pum-pum..." This Christmas the holly pricks –
my gift must be a loved old man.

Japanese Garden

This mud was meant to be a garden.
School children planted trees;
youths on a Government scheme
arranged rocks,
laid out sand.
Now the pond is thick with ice,
the bridges are broken.
What vandals did not destroy,
our climate has contorted.

There is tranquillity here, even so.
The carp stone rises to Heaven;
beauty hovers between frozen reeds
and Winter sun. Beyond the fence,
a hockey whistle blows,
but here there is rest.
My feet crunch ice.
From the hawthorn,
a robin lifts in silent flight.

The Japanese were a warlike people,
yet they preserved such places.
Their Samurai must have stood,
as I stand now, thinking of time:
the burning days,
the peasant lugging his life.
Through the lines of rock and water,
they saw the eternal, and found relief.
Briefly, I share their peace.

Outbreak of War

My day passes with the scent of cake.
I break an egg into a well of flour
and listen as the radio states:
"Last ditch attempt at peace."
Next Tuesday, war may begin.
Experts talk of pre-emptive strikes;
I line and grease a baking tray.

If asked, I would warn
that skin, like eggshell, is thin
and will smash when struck by steel.
No one seeks my opinion,
though they may well require my son.
So, folding currants into yellow paste,
I watch them sink, like soldiers into sand.

Work must be done, whatever the news.
The labourer tilled his field
while Napoleon camped beyond his hedge.
As Anthony and Cleopatra fought,
their slaves went on chiselling.
Tomorrow, I shall buy extra bread,
and candles, in case the lights go out.

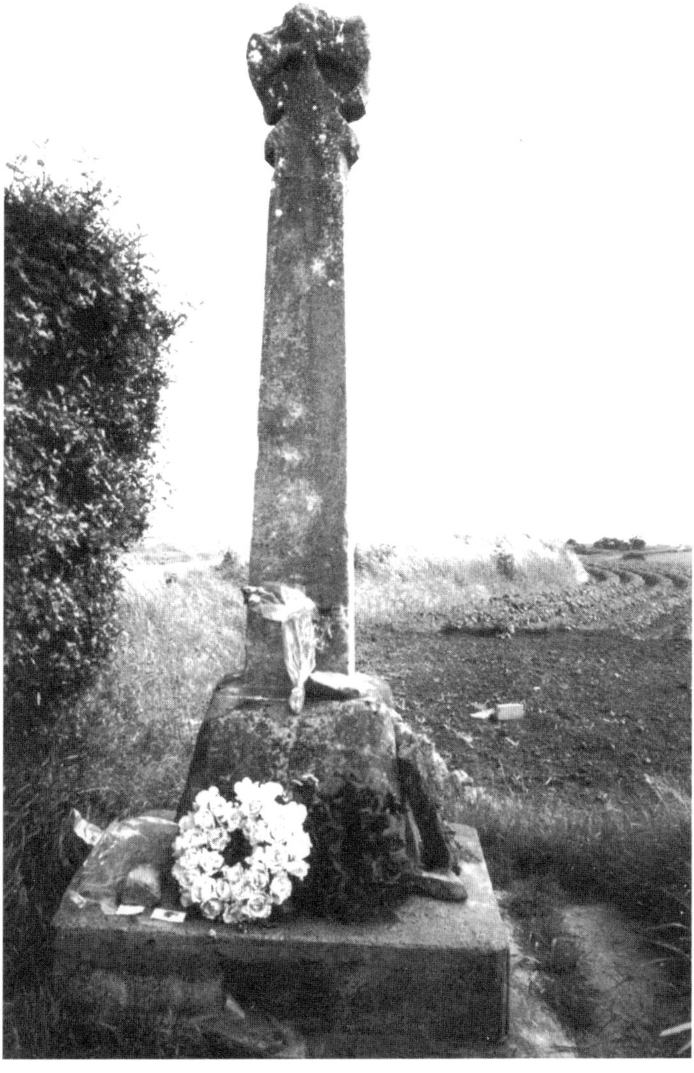

Refugees

When do we leave –
Cancel the milk, stop the papers?
There are whispers on the train
And letters go astray.
We are not wanted here.

Once, we were decent folk,
Growing a little stout,
Respecting the law and the neighbours.
We cast our vote, when we remembered,
And forgot it decently afterwards.

Now waiters refuse to serve us
And the school has no places.
The man on the street shouts hate
Not news, and our parties are invaded
By black-shirted men.

Perhaps we should pack our cases.
But where should we go? And how?
The wind blows cold across the station.
Who would want us, anyway –
Decent folk, growing a little stout?

War Cemetery

We pay our ten pence, take a card
and walk through silence, past
a marble corpse, dead centre in a deadly space.
The sun touches rows of graves,
glints on silver birch, yellows yellowing leaves.

My mind cannot translate sums
that question arithmetic. How many?
Almost five thousand ... dying on English soil,
and buried here on Cannock Chase.
Erich Faust UFFZ,

Konrad Rudowski, OBLT...
Four to the slab they lie, two names to the front,
two at the back, in letters carefully measured,
spaced, chiselled. Anton, Georg,
Gerardus, Hermann ...

Names and rank bewilder, dazzle
in English sun. A few frail posies
splash colour against regimental stones.
Who came here to place their roses,
these dying chrysanths?

Anton, Georg, Gerardus, Hermann ...
And just as neatly, laid out in German fields,
Anthony, George, Gerald, Harry lie.
Separated by a narrow sea,
their graves glint in September sun.

Crocuses

Despair crouched, like a gargoyle
at the corner of her mind,
soot clothed, fingers to mouth.

An April northerly had moaned
all night, bending the trees,
blighting hopes like seeds.

Then suddenly on a verge
where mud and ice seeped
still, there was joy, blowing.

Crocuses:
purple and yellow,
an ambush of delight.

Brief Magic

It arrives so quickly –
      suddenly, the dawn is full of singing,
swifts circle a powder-blue sky.
      Green is back in fashion,
lawnmowers beat rallentando.

It offers so sweetly –
      a touch of warmth on your skin,
the taste of candy floss bought at a fair.
      For a few honeyed weeks
vicars serve strawberries and cream.

We drink each day greedily,
      savour the flavour of freedom.
A Northern Summer passes so quickly,
      brief magic granted to
those who know our Winter's night.

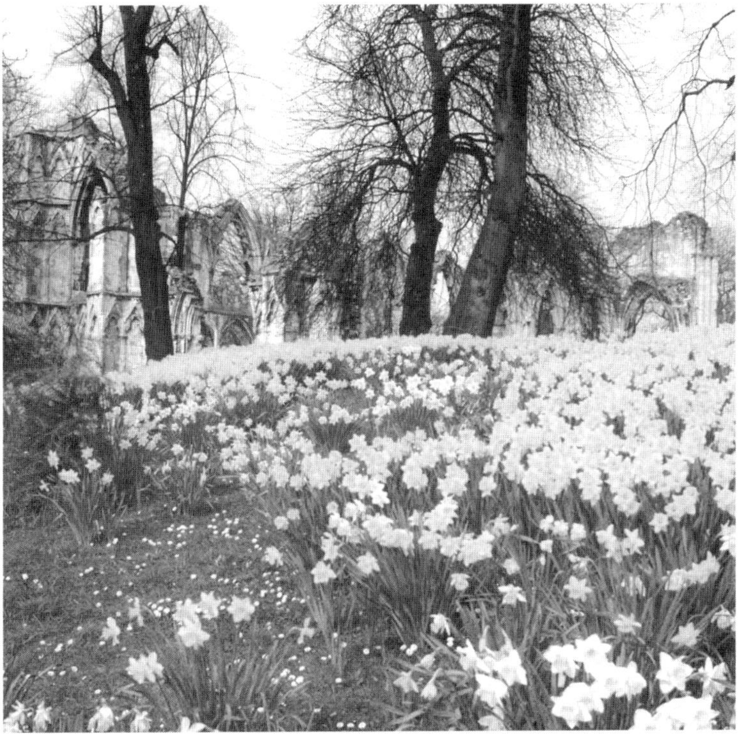

Pet Blessing

The poodle requires a seat in the choir,
Tim's Scottie has designs on the Vicar.
This is pet blessing at Lotherton Hall.
Borrow a hymn sheet and sing to the band.

In no other county, in no other land
could you find such a mixture –
of absurdity and fine music,
reverence and good humour.

Vicky's cat is singing Te Deum,
Richard's goldfish prays in its bowl.
The courtyard is splendidly decayed,
but the custom we follow is much older.

Once the milch cow and rooster were brought
to placate the gods and seek fertility.
Now we ask blessings on tortoise and budgie,
and wonder if next door's cat has been spayed.

Who cares? Dad's fetched the ice-cream,
the bab's asleep and the bills can wait.
Take out your video and record the scene.
Sing hey for Yorkshire, hey for Tradition,

Sing hey, for Summer!

Reflections

Today
the world has inverted.
Mountains float downwards,
trees reach up to pebbles,
plait reeds, frame setting sun.
A swan glides beneath its shadow,
clouds slide beyond my feet.

For one rare,
tranquil moment, nothing
disturbs a mirrored afternoon.
I am Alice, in Looking Glass Land.
If I move very slowly, my other self
and I may clasp fingers,
across a universe.

Mijas, Spain

Patroness, doll, goddess,
image of sanctity,
the Virgen de la Peña watches.
Restrained by golden chains
buckets of carnations jostle,
climb her altar steps. Patiently
she looks down, in triangular dress,
a very unenglish Madonna.
The pilgrims enter, whisper, pray;
ordinary people.
One checks a mobile phone.

Such devotion is like the flowers,
too much for me. I was taught to wrap God tight,
and lay Him out in a Victorian box.
Grandad interpreted Revelations;
visitors predicted the Second Coming,
or the dangers of sex and too much chocolate.
For us, Pleasure was of the Flesh, and the Flesh
an ill-fitting coat, soon to be shed.
Flowers stayed straight, jammed into mesh
in chapel vases.

As I grew up though,
I found warmer places
where other relatives talked too loud
and boasted of cars they did not own.
In our family you either took to religion
or drink. Some uncles managed both.
I learnt to fear extremes,
and remember the neighbours.

Candles and gold madonnas
belonged to foreign places,
like sunshine and risky food.
Now, in March heat,
We take photographs, pose
before bell tower and sanctuary.

Above us, a white figure of Christ
offers his bleeding heart, while
a taxi rank of donkey carts shuffles.

The afternoon echoes with voices;
History beats relentlessly,
like the sun.
Romans fortified this place
but on Turdetan foundations.
Moslems conquered, to flee
eight centuries later.
All that time Mijas remained true
to a reign beyond the mountains,
and a faith buried in this grotto.

The legend is stranger than the Madonna:
that a pigeon led two startled boys
into this cave, to find the virgin's image
revealed in beauty, miraculously.
Ever since, pilgrims have come,
like the flowers soon faded,
but continually replaced.

To hold to such a story -
the dream tempts, but I doubt
if even the pilgrims believe it nowadays.
As they return to their offices and bars
how do they square a triangular Madonna?

Yet they achieve some resolution,
which is more than I have done,
building an arch of words above
a nothingness I fear, and cannot accept.
I need such places as this; this quiet courtyard
in troubled years, this beauty, these legends
disbelieved, but loved. As our bus rattles down
to darkening cities, the sanctuary is still sunlit,
set firm on its promontory,
still looking out over vineyards and houses,
and bewildering views.

Feather

Trodden in the leaf litter,
it is no more than
a relic from an ageing bird.
Then the child stoops,

claims it as her own.
To her, it is the magic quill
that wrote the spell of Autumn:
pearl smooth, translucent.

To her biologist father
it is a moment's aid, evidence
of wing shape and type,
perfection in barb and keratin.

To the bird itself, it is life,
skin, bone, flight, courtship,
pride. And yet it remains
- a feather.

Hymn

God gives a new, wonderful world
To those who share His grace;
He grants the seasons' joys to hold
And with them, shows us peace.

The shimmer of a summer's heat
The flies that dance above,
The leaves that fall and smell so sweet,
All teach our Father's love.

Ev'n the storm that tears all night
And Winter's cold so long -
They shout their joy at nature's might,
And guide us through their song.

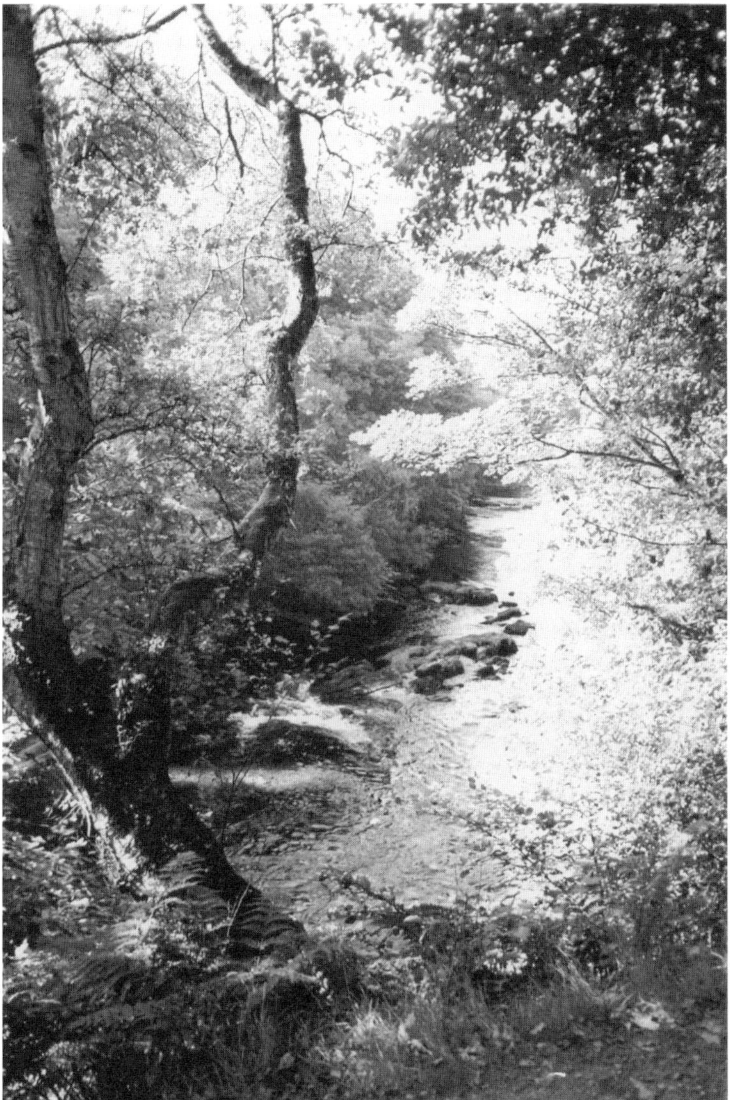

Benediction
(for a wedding)

May the music of your love
play sweetly, play softly,
yet strongly, prelude to a lifetime.

May your separate notes weave
surely around and between you,
like a fine tapestry.

May your voices together
blend, neither seeking dominance,
but finding harmony

as the discords of Life
resolve for you into melody,
though the tone and tempo vary.

And, as the years dance by,
your progress will be amaroso –
never strident or off-key -

until this day's happiness
becomes first movement
in a symphony of joy.

Faith Tea

"Faith Tea this Saturday.
Speaker Miss Ivy Harbottle."
Driving past the sign I smiled.
Do they still have Faith Teas?

All the way down the road
I was getting ready for tea and faith,
with a bow in my hair big enough
for wings, and Dad fastening his cuffs,
while the gas fire spluttered and the cat
swung on Mum's corset laces.
Spirella did well in those days,
before ladies let it all hang out.

Those were simpler times,
or so they seem now.
We used to walk into the chapel
knowing why we were there: for faith
and angel cakes, both thought good
for building you up. Now cakes
are suspect, being high in cholesterol,
and faith is circumspect, admitted
only between consenting adults.

Would I return to those days?
A simpler past has its attraction
viewed from a morning traffic jam,
and I have almost forgotten
the piano was off key and the buns,
like the ladies who served them,
ample but of undetermined age.
Still, I doubt if I'd settle.
My life has sprawled too much
to cram into a simple faith,
or a girdle.

Other Publications by Pauline Kirk

Poetry collections: *Walking to Snailbeach: Selected and New Poems*, Redbeck Press, 2004; *Owlstone*, Thalia Press, 2002; *No Cure in Tears*, Aireings Publications, 1997; *Travelling Solo*, K.T. Publications, 1995; *Rights of Way*, Unibird Press, 1990; *Red Marl and Brick*, Littlewood Press, 1985; *Scorpion Days*, Rivelin Press, 1982 and Medal Poets Australia, 1987.

Novels: *The Keepers*, Virago (Little, Brown), 1996 and 1997; *Waters of Time*, Century Hutchinson 1988; Ulverscroft 1991.

Editorial work and Criticism: *Fighting Cocks – Forty Years of Pennine Poets: SPIRIT AND EMOTION*, Mabel Ferrett, and *MIND AND BODY*, K.E.Smith, both Fighting Cock Press, 2006 (supported by Arts Council England, Yorkshire); *Brian Merrikin Hill: Poet and Mentor*, Fighting Cock Press, 1999; *The Fairy Band*, Walter Hill, KT Publications, 1997; *Streets Ahead: The Castleford Renewal Experience*, Yorkshire Art Circus, 1994 (with Brian Lewis); *A Survivor Myself: Experiences of Child Abuse*, Yorkshire Art Circus 1994; *Bramley: the Village that Disappeared*, Bramley History Society, 1983 with subsequent reprints; other community and local history booklets. Senior Editor, Fighting Cock Press.